Dear Parent:

Congratulations! Your child is taking the first steps on an exciting journey. The destination? Independent reading!

STEP INTO READING® will help your child get there. The program offers five steps to reading success. Each step includes fun stories and colorful art. There are also Step into Reading Sticker Books, Step into Reading Math Readers, Step into Reading Write-In Readers, Step into Reading Phonics Readers, and Step into Reading Phonics First Steps! Boxed Sets—a complete literacy program with something for every child.

Learning to Read, Step by Step!

Ready to Read   Preschool–Kindergarten
• big type and easy words • rhyme and rhythm • picture clues
For children who know the alphabet and are eager to begin reading.

Reading with Help   Preschool–Grade 1
• basic vocabulary • short sentences • simple stories
For children who recognize familiar words and sound out new words with help.

Reading on Your Own   Grades 1–3
• engaging characters • easy-to-follow plots • popular topics
For children who are ready to read on their own.

Reading Paragraphs   Grades 2–3
• challenging vocabulary • short paragraphs • exciting stories
For newly independent readers who read simple sentences with confidence.

Ready for Chapters   Grades 2–4
• chapters • longer paragraphs • full-color art
For children who want to take the plunge into chapter books but still like colorful pictures.

STEP INTO READING® is designed to give every child a successful reading experience. The grade levels are only guides. Children can progress through the steps at their own speed, developing confidence in their reading, no matter what their grade.

Remember, a lifetime love of reading starts with a

D0197044

To Eric Siegel
—L.R.P.

Photos courtesy of: © CORBIS (p. 37). © Meijert de Haan/epa/CORBIS (p. 25).
© Jim Edds/CORBIS (p. 46). © Warren Faidley/CORBIS (p. 13; pp. 42-43). © Sally A. Morgan/
Ecoscene/CORBIS (p. 28). © Eric Nguyen/CORBIS (p. 12). © Jim Reed/CORBIS (p. 18). ©
Reuters/CORBIS (cover).

Published in the United States by Random House Children's Books, a division of Random
House, Inc., New York. The text of this work was originally published in the United States
by Random House Children's Books in 1996.

Step into Reading, Random House, and the Random House colophon are
registered trademarks of Random House, Inc.

Visit us on the Web!
www.stepintoreading.com

Educators and librarians, for a variety of teaching tools, visit us at
www.randomhouse.com/teachers

Library of Congress Cataloging-in-Publication Data
Penner, Lucille Recht.
Twisters! / by Lucille Recht Penner ; illustrated by Allen Garns.
   p.   cm.
ISBN 978-0-375-86224-3 (trade) — ISBN 978-0-375-96224-0 (lib. bdg.)
1. Tornadoes—Juvenile literature. I. Garns, Allen, ill. II. Title.
QC955.2.P463 2009
551.55'3—dc22
2009003866

Printed in the United States of America
10 9 8 7 6 5

STEP INTO READING®

STEP 3

Twisters!

By Lucille Recht Penner

Illustrated by Allen Garns

Random House 🏠 New York

On a summer afternoon,
a train chugged through fields
of golden wheat.
Suddenly, thunder crashed.
A whirling black cloud
swooped down toward the tracks.

The engineer
looked out his window.
That whirling cloud
was a twister,
and he was heading
right into it!
It was too late to stop!

The twister ripped off
the cab's steel roof.
Wind clawed at the man.
He grabbed his chair,
closed his eyes,
and held on.

Suddenly, the wind stopped.

The engineer opened his eyes.

The sky was clear.

The train had passed

right through the twister!

That twister was a tornado.

A tornado is one of the strongest forces

on Earth.

It can pick up
a car or a house.

Tornadoes can even rip

somebody's clothes off.

The United States
has more tornadoes
than anywhere else.
Most of them
hit the Midwest
in an area called Tornado Alley.
This is a place where cold air
coming down from Canada
collides with warm air
coming up from
the Gulf of Mexico.

As the warm air rises,

it punches a hole

in the cold air.

Up the warm air swirls

in a long column.

The column of swirling air
begins to look
like a funnel
hanging from the sky.

If the funnel
touches the ground,
it's a tornado.

Tornadoes seem crazy.
Sometimes they smash
whatever they touch.
But once a tornado
lifted a crate of eggs
and carried it
half a mile.
It put the crate
down gently.
Not a single egg
was broken!

Another tornado
lifted the roof
off a schoolhouse.
Children were blown
out of their chairs.
They landed hundreds
of feet away.
Luckily, no one
was badly hurt.

Most tornadoes are
over in minutes.
But one tornado
lasted four hours.
It tore up towns
along its path
through Missouri, Illinois,
and Indiana.

A farmer in Illinois
saw green paper
fall out of the sky.
It was money!
The tornado had
carried it from a town
a hundred miles away.

Most tornadoes strike
in the afternoon or early evening
in spring and summer.
The National Weather Service
issues a "tornado watch"
if there's a chance that
a tornado is likely to form.

A "tornado warning"
is more serious.
It means a tornado
has already formed.
The warning goes out
over radio and television.
Sirens blow and wail.
Take cover!

The safest place
to take cover
is a storm cellar.
It's a special
underground room.

If you don't
have a storm cellar,
you should go down
into your basement.
If you don't have
a basement either,
hide in a closet
with no outside walls.

One family hid in a closet

as a tornado

roared overhead.

When the wind died down,
they opened the closet door.
The rest of their house was gone!

Tornadoes can make
a loud, scary noise
like a million buzzing bees.

Most tornadoes form over land.
Twisters that form over water
are called "waterspouts."
Waterspouts can suck
all the water
out of a pond.
They can suck up
frogs, tadpoles, and fish.

A waterspout once
dropped hundreds of fish
on a town in Louisiana.
Everyone ran outside.
The streets were covered
with fresh fish.
Some were still alive
and flopping around.

Another kind of twister
sometimes forms in the desert.
It's called a "dust devil."
Hot air rises, whipping up
a spiral of sand and dust.
It looks like someone
doing a wild dance.
Some dust devils
are little.
Some are a thousand feet high!

In Tucson, Arizona,
a dust devil pulled
the roof off a house.
It came down
across the street.

Tornadoes, waterspouts,

and dust devils

are never more than a mile wide.

Hurricanes are much bigger.

Hurricane winds blow in circles

that can be hundreds

of miles across.

At the center

is an area

called the hurricane's "eye."

In the eye,

the air is calm.

The sun may shine.

But around it,

the wind blows

faster and faster.

The first hurricane each year

is given a name starting

with the letter A.

The second hurricane

gets a B name.

Boys' and girls' names

take turns.

Agnes, Bob, and Carol

were all famous hurricanes.

Hurricanes form over oceans.
Their powerful winds
push the sea into waves.
The water swells up in a huge bump
called a storm surge.
When a hurricane comes ashore,
the storm surge can
wash away beaches.
It can even cut islands
in half!

In 1900, a great storm
struck Galveston, Texas.
The wind rose suddenly.
People stood on the beach,
amazed at the sight
of the huge waves.
Isaac Cline,
the chief weather forecaster,
raced up and down
with a horse and buggy.

"Get back," he shouted.

"It's a hurricane!"

Suddenly, the storm surge
swept over the beach
and poured into the city.
More than 6,000 people
died in the storm.

The dead bodies of people and animals
floated through the streets.

Isaac Cline's warning
had come too late.

Now the National Weather Service
tracks hurricanes
with weather satellites.

It warns people
to leave the coast
if a hurricane is coming.
Shelters are set up
in buildings inland.
People can stay there
until the storm passes.

In 1969, the Weather Service
issued a warning.
Hurricane Camille was coming!
Thousands of people fled inland.
The early warning saved their lives.
But people in one apartment house
decided to stay
and watch the storm.

Camille's winds smashed into land
at 170 miles per hour!
Its storm surge
destroyed the building.
Eight people died.

In 1992, part of Florida
was changed forever.
Hurricane Andrew
washed away beaches,
knocked down bridges,
and wiped out whole towns.

But almost everyone escaped.
Again, the warning
had come in time.
Although Andrew destroyed
thousands of homes,
only 39 people were killed.

Twisters are scary.
Most people run away
from them.
But "storm chasers"
want to see storms close-up
and photograph them.
Storm chasers drive vans
with video cameras
on the roof.

If a tornado
gets too close,
the vans can go
very fast.
It's dangerous work!
Only an expert
should chase a tornado.

Air force pilots

fly right into hurricanes

to measure their

size, speed, and direction.

They fly special planes

called "hurricane hunters."

It's strange inside

a hurricane.

Sometimes the pilot

doesn't even know

if he's right side up

or upside down.

He can only tell

from his instruments.

A tornado can
knock down buildings
faster than a wrecker's ball.

A great hurricane
has the power
of a hydrogen bomb.

Scientists,
hurricane hunters,
and storm chasers
are learning the secrets
of twisters and hurricanes.
And the more we know,
the safer we will be.